Love and Lies Do Not Mix

CW00881539

Pete Frierson

Order this book online at www.trafford.com
or email orders@trafford.com

Most Trafford titles are also available at major online book retailers.

Print information available on the last page.

ISBN: 978-1-4907-9381-8 (sc)
ISBN: 978-1-4907-9380-1 (e)

Library of Congress Control Number: 2019934301

Our mission is to efficiently provide the world's finest, most comprehensive book publishing service, enabling every author to experience success. To find out how to publish your book, your way, and have it available worldwide, visit us online at www.trafford.com

Trafford rev. 02/20/2019

Trafford
PUBLISHING®   www.trafford.com
North America & international
toll-free: 1 888 232 4444 (USA & Canada)
fax: 812 355 4082

Love and Lies
Do Not Mix

To my colleagues in the legal field. Also to Master Chief Eric L. Harp; Dr. Harry and Pat Coleman; Ronald and Bernice Ryan; Jerry and Peggy Tanner; Carlos and Christian Eason; Marla Williams; Janet Mymatt; Cherrelle Hopper; Anna Catlin; Berrie Boyd; Janice Troop; Ashten Kegler; Becky Horton; James Horton; Harold and Lydia Williams; Roger G. Brown; Tracy Woodall; Cathy Young Monroe; Angeline G. Butler, Carmichael Kemp; Sammy Abernathy; Pat Mock; Emory and Gerri Lee; Russell and Erik Overby; Charlie Fisher; Terrance Pride; Patrick Carter; Dana Dye; Allston Vander Horst; Judge Stella L. Hargrove; Judge Russell Parkes; Judge J. Lee Bailey III; Judge David L. Allen; Marteza Frierson; Pete Frierson, Jr.; Alisha Smith Frierson and my grandchildren, Sydney, Siraj and Sanaa; The late Wilnita K. Hardiman, Chief James Boyd, Pat Troop, John and Louise McClain, James Garner, my parents-Clarence and Alma Frierson and my brother, Clarence Frierson, Jr.

CONTENTS

ACKNOWLEDGMENTS

Without the support of my team, my book would not have come to fruition. *Love and Lies Do Not Mix* shows how love and emotions can change lives in an instant if they are not nurtured or cultivated the way love is intended.

I take this opportunity to thank Diane Davis, Diane James, Kathy L. Hardiman, and Debora Lambert for making *Love and Lies Do Not Mix* an intriguing and masterful work to be presented to the world. Special thanks to all of you who have supported my previous books and given me words of encouragement.

The word "love" is the most powerful four letters in this universe when it comes together as God has intended. May you enjoy the thoughts of your heart, body, mind, and soul while reading this book.

Love and Lies Do Not Mix is written to entice the readers to the realization that love can be both a beautiful and not-so-good life experience. My desire is to show the good and the not so good in love.

Life itself can be a challenge. However, we look for one common thread in life, that is, to find real love with good experiences if possible. I hope the reader will realize that my writings portray what human beings experience throughout their lives with and without love. Once we learn to accept a challenge and we face it head on, then we will begin to recover and look forward to a wonderful, loving, enjoyable, and exciting life.

I hope that you will be inspired by what you read and be able to reflect on your life or of someone that you know who has experienced love in a wonderful way and otherwise.

DEAR

My friend Dear has transcended into the world of happiness with the Lord, where she never worries anymore, no more phone calls for assistance knowing only a few faithful will respond.

I love her dearly like so many others. She had a spirit that would rock the world. She loved to give folks nicknames, for they were always fitting to that person. Who could not love this gentle, sweet, loving white-haired lady? She was loved by most and feared by others.

Dear, you have left a few of us behind to fight your battles, and we will do just that. You have warned us of the fight after you have transcended, and it hasn't taken long. Your love and your wisdom will carry us through.

Fly like an eagle and do not stop until you arrive in heaven. Say hello to all my loved ones and those you may not even know. Goodbye, my sweet, loving gray-headed lady. With love forever and a day.

MY BEST FRIEND, LESOM

I can remember all the things that we used to do as shipmates. Most were good, and some were not so good. But we made a promise to each other that we would be friends until the end.

The end for me is death. We have shared things that we have done, good or bad. You are my best friend.

So the question may be to some, what is a best friend? The answer is simple to me. A best friend is someone who will be there with you to the end. No matter the situation or time of day or night, your best friend will be there. A best friend is someone who will drop everything that they are doing to be at your bedside, if that is the situation. A best friend knows what you think, what you like, and what you want more so than others.

You are my best friend, and you will be my best friend until the end.

Sometimes life situations and distance can cause the fiber to stretch between two best friends, but never shall the fiber break. If you have a best friend—and you only need one—keep that friend until the end. In today's world, people can't write, can't call, can't send a card; then just send a text and say, "You are my best friend."

No matter where you go, no matter what you do, no matter which way life takes you, just always remember that you are my best friend, and no one on this earth can separate the two of us because you are my best friend to the end.

MY GRANDDAUGHTER

My granddaughter is only five years old, but she is filled with love, joy, and excitement. At times, when she is not on her iPad, she might have a conversation with her grand P. She will listen and then—yes, at five—give me her opinion, and wow. Sometimes I have to say, "Son, translate what she just said." But that's my granddaughter.

My granddaughter is the last one that's expected in this clan, so I have to spend as much time as possible with her. Now that her words are clearer, all I hear is Grand P this and Grand P that. "Let's go outside or see what's on my iPad." She has never stopped once, but that's my granddaughter. I love her more than life itself. I don't see much of her, but when I do, it's fun, fun, and fun.

I LOVE YOU

I love you for who you are, but there are many other reasons too. It could be something that you have said or something that you have done. It could be the way you talk to me or listen to me. I love you because of your smile and not your frown.

I love you because two hearts have come together, and however that may have happened, a relationship begins. Every day will not be like a rose garden, but I love you even when there are a few sticky thorns. I love you in the warmest way because there is no other way to love you.

I love you because I care from the deepest part of my fiber, and nothing can change that wonderful feeling that I have for you that causes me to love you, love you, and love you. I love you when you are in the room and when you are not there. I love you when I am lying around with nothing to do, but have you on my mind, in my heart, and in my soul. I love you not for who you are, but because of the person you have evolved into, a person I have never dreamed will stand by me. I love you.

I love you from the moment I laid eyes on you and until the day my eyes are closed forever. I will always love you through the good and the not-so-good times. I love you. I will always love you, you, and you until the end of time.

LIFE CHANGES

"Life changes" is such an interesting topic that you have to follow along with me to understand. Life changes are what it is really all about. As we enter this world, we have no idea how we are going out.

From the time we begin to grow, we see things through our eyes, and we determine whatever it may be. Life changes or life in general will bring about a transformation; it can be for the best or for the worst. We program ourselves for the positive things in life and not the negative, but again, life will bring about changes.

Life brings about changes that are so beautiful and so wonderful that we can hardly imagine that it is meant for us, but then life can also throw us a curve. However, we learn in this old world that we must adapt to whatever changes that are placed before us.

Changes, just what do they mean? Changes in life, for the most part, are a gradual thing, and sometimes a degree of maturity comes with it. When we go through something, we hope to come out stronger like never before, but those are changes as well.

Changes—some are small, some big, and really some not at all. We have to adapt to make it in the world. Life changes from day to day, situation to situation, but one thing remains the same—people cause life changes sometimes for the best and other times for the worse. You can be the judge.

Jobs can cause a life change, folks moving in and out, and sometimes the general environment can cause life changes. They are a part of living in this old world. Just think, if everything remained the same, this old world would be boring.

Life changes—accept them. Make the best of each day. Never give up and remain positive regardless of life changes.

LIFE EXPERIENCES

We have many experiences in life. Some are good ones, and we look forward to those. However, some of our experiences are not so good, and it leaves a mark on our souls.

Bad experiences sometimes translate into an encounter of a lifetime, and we sometimes have difficulties trying to get past the bad ones. More often than not, I hear folks talk about life experiences where the word "love" comes into play. Whether it be marriage, relationships, family, or others, the word "love" comes into play.

I would hope that we take the good and make it better. We take the bad and improve on it. One bad experience does not have to be a lifetime of mental and emotional entrapment. However, we know that happens quite often, and then we spend a lifetime of misery, which is not necessary in today's world.

Life experiences should be like taking a day at a time, especially when we know where we have come from and where we are going and when we determine that no one is going to stop us. We can get over life experiences, and there are going to be many. All I say to those out there who may be going through something is this: that something can only be determined by you. If it is a bad experience, change it; and if it is a good one, make it better and enjoy life to the fullest because, after all, you only come this way once.

LIFE

Life is a place of being, hoping we can share moments of happiness on the highway or byway. Life is so precious yet taken so lightly. Today I love you, and tomorrow I'm gone. Life is a place of being.

Life is like no other; once gone, it's gone. Somehow we embrace the world around us to laugh, to cry, and sometimes to jump for joy.

Life is a learning experience with the smell of roses or the sound of hard knocks.

Life is eternal, for we find ourselves searching our inner thoughts to see and remind us, we are human with love and feelings, yet life remains internal.

Life is like folklore. It's what one chooses to make of it. Sometimes we question our pure existence, yet we learn to roll with the punches and dance with the music.

Life is everlasting. We love to create the memories of yesterdays and yesteryears. Life is filled with memories, stories, love, sadness, happiness, hope, and the everlasting sense of "untold stories." Life is today, tomorrow, and the future.

So now we have it. Life is learning. Life is eternal. Life is folklore. Life is everlasting. Life shall always remain when one person decides their mode of operation—love, life, and happiness forever.

EXCITEMENT

Excitement of life can be a variety of things. As human beings, we become excited about life, love, family, friends, promotions, something new, and life itself. Excitement is something that reminds me of love. Good love will always bring a smile to our face and laughter to our heart. Excitement can do the same thing.

Excitement can be designed in many ways, depending on the perception of the person receiving and being a part of the excitement.

Have you ever brought something that you truly want, and then all of sudden you receive it, and you become so excited that it kind of reminds you of a baby with a new toy? You just don't know what to do with it but enjoy it.

Excitement, what does that mean? I am hoping that it brings joy to the heart, relief to the soul, and appeasement to the mind. No matter which type of excitement that you receive in your life, learn to enjoy it because today or tomorrow is not promised.

LIFE TRAVELS

Life's travels are a great thing. We travel here and there. Long and short distances are all life's travels. Life can be so much fun. We see things in a different light. Kids laugh, adults plan, and the rest, we just let it run.

What a way to go. Arizona, Tennessee, North Carolina, South Carolina, Georgia, Colorado—there are many other ways to travel and see the world in another light.

Sometimes what we do today affects us for a lifetime. Life's travels, I wouldn't give them up for a million dollars. Our life travels are just that—life travels.

LOVE IS A FOUR-LETTER WORD

"Love" is a four-letter word that is so powerful that even the human mind does not understand all the twists and turns, trials and tribulations, ups and downs, the smooth and the rough, but it is love. "Love" is a powerful four-letter word.

Love is something that we all look forward to. Love, in its truest form, can cause a variety of reactions. It could be love from a daughter, son, husband, wife, lover, soul mate, partner, or many other aspects of life.

We learn to cultivate love where we are comfortable. When we rest at night, we smile with such intensity that we know love is in the air. "Love" is a powerful four-letter word that will follow us all the days of our life while here on the earth.

Learn to enjoy life. Learn to live. Learn to love to the fullest.

OUR LOVE

Our love is forever, thanks to God.
We stood the test and came out stronger.
We are more determined than ever to make this love work.
Days sometimes seem like weeks,
and now each day is a
day of love filled with happiness.
There is some truth to miracles.
I believe with all my heart that to love,
to honor, to respect, to commit, to share, and to always be honest will
make true love live forever.
I believe in God Almighty, and knowing He is in the mix will guide, protect, and show me to trust Him
and the person whom I love.

We survived the crack in the foundation, but it never really broke completely, and now
that foundation of love is stronger than ever.
My cup can runneth over
with love at any time because God is with us.
To a new beginning
that will always be focused on each other and God.

From me to you and from you to me, I love you with all my heart.
Thank you, thank you, and thank you.

THERE IS SO MUCH LOVE IN MY HEART FOR YOU

There is much love in my heart for you. The way you look at me melts my heart to the core. The way that you touch me gives me such a warm, loving sensation. The way you hold me shows just how much you love me. The way you smile at me lets me know there is much love in my heart for you.

There is much love in my heart for you. Even when there are no roses on the table, my love grows for you. Even in times of despair, my love grows for you. Even when we do not see things the same, my love grows for you. Even when the sun turns dark, my love still grows for you. This goes to show that there is much love in my heart for you.

There is much love in my heart for you from the day that I met you, and as the years roll by, my love still grows for you. I cannot think how my life will be without you because I love you so deeply. I am only human, and so are you. Our nights will become lonely, but our love will continue to grow. Again, there is much love in my heart for you.

YOU ARE THE JOY OF MY LIFE

You are the joy of my life, not only for today, but forever. We spent years building a love that could exist between the two of us.

You are the joy of my life each minute of the day. Your love has carried me down mountains, through valleys, around corners, and through the unknown. You are the joy of my life.

I feel like there is nothing that I cannot do because of the love I have for you. Your warm smile gives me inspiration when I am down, and your touch lifts me up over and over again.

You are the joy of my life daily, and never allow anyone to tell you otherwise. My actions are worth a million kisses and hugs because you know and feel the love I have for you. You are the joy of my life. I love you more than words can ever say.

THOSE WHO CARE—LOVE MATTERS

Those who care about one another with love and show it openly and unconditionally demonstrate an unusual characteristic that can blend and strengthen love, life, and relationships for a lifetime. Caring is another way to show love. It has ways of transforming romance into a peaceful spirit of happiness to the heart, body, mind, and soul.

Those who care can help the weak become strong and uplift those who needs uplifting, yet loving that special person in your life unconditionally. Love bonds where nothing else does. Love reaches deeper than life itself.

Love really matters, and with you, that's all that matters to me. I am one of those who care about you. I care because of the way you love me and how you show and express your love to me. It's like this: Love matters not today but tomorrow. Love matters because without your love, I will be suffering in silence. Love matters because I can feel what I have been missing, and that belongs to and is a part of something so beautiful that only comes once in a lifetime. Love matters because without your love, joy will not come in the morning and evening, and joy won't have meaning.

Love matters, and your entire well-being belongs to me and God. Thank you for caring. Thank you for loving me.

Whatever storm that we must weather, we will do it together because care and love matters. And you matter the most to me.

You are what I have waited for, for a lifetime, and we will not lose each other because love matters to us. I will always be by your side. My spirit lives within you forever.

WHY ME, LORD?

Why me Lord, I don't know. Many things have happened to me, but I still carry on. The pain, the tears, the hurt, the uncertainty, and the unknown make me say, "Why me, Lord?"

Why me Lord, your love for thee keeps me going day in and day out, never giving up. Having you on my side makes life easier, even for me to say, "Why me, Lord?"

DATES IN OUR LIVES

Many things happen in our lifetime, and there will be dates that we will always remember, including the day of the week, the time, and what happened. Dates are important because, as we grow older, we like to recall those positive events and things.

It was a fall month and a warm day when love, happiness, peace, and a lifetime commitment was recovered.

The world waits for the love, happiness, peace, and commitment of people who truly love each other. When love touches lives in the right way, anything is possible, but one thing is for sure—you can tell the difference between true love and the feeling of what we think might be love.

Your touch, your smile, your eyes, and the mere presence of love cannot be measured by anyone but those who know and feel the love. True love is a feeling never felt before and will always be felt by the mind, heart, body, and soul. Saying "I love you" can be so powerful in the art of true love and happiness.

Dates are so important, such as how, when, and where we met; our first kiss; the first time we made love; and even all those small things that we do to enhance our forever love. As the years come and go, our love lives on and on. Our hearts remain young, and our thoughts are forever focused on each other.

So like any day that starts and comes to an end, never forget what true love can do for the heart, mind, body, and soul, just pure happiness that cannot be purchased in a store. It's only from the love of each other. Let's love each other as if this were the last day on the earth. I love you, I love you, and I just love you.

DAYS COME AND DAYS GO

Days come and days go, but weekends are forever, just you and me. Wow, it makes life worth living. Weekends or just a weekend, every now and then, represents the love of two people smiling and laughing.

It's just a weekend to share, to talk, to move mountains, and to allow love to flow above, below, and just around us. It's a weekend where memories are made, promises are kept, and the unexpected appears with a pleasant surprise. It's just a weekend to say, "I love you, dear." It's just a weekend never to come back around, so we do this, and we do that. It's just a weekend with a glow never shown before.

It's just a weekend. Baby, I want you to know every day of my life, I live for the next weekend. It's just a weekend in a world of love and happiness, together for today, tomorrow, and forever. It's just a weekend to say again, "I love you more each day." It's just a weekend suited for just you and me. Love is just a weekend away.

CHANGES

We have to adapt to changes. The mind allows us to adapt. Some of us can, and some of us can't. Some fall, and some rise; others succeed, and others fail, but life will bring about changes.

Changes depend really on how you perceive them. If you have had a change in your life, no matter what it may be and sometimes there may be plenty, learn to accept them and keep it rolling because, after all, from the day that we are born until the day we transcend to the other world, we will go through many different changes; and hopefully, you will realize that not all changes are bad.

Changes could be good for the heart, body, mind, and soul, not to mention the spirit. Without our spirit, which is within us, we are lost. Adapt, enjoy, and accept whatever changes that are put before you, and be grateful that you have lived a long life where you can accept changes no matter what.

CALM ME IF YOU WILL

Living in a world of uncertainty where nothing seems to remain the same, calm me if you will. Sometimes things seem so calm, and then something small upsets the calmness and make waves like the aftermath of a storm. Calm me if you will.

Then your touch calms the waves, smooths away the storm, brings out the sunshine, and puts love back where it belongs. Calm me if you will. Trying to stay on track is my goal, allowing nothing to steal my joy.

Your touch, your look, your smile, your words have just delivered the calmness of my life. Calm me if you will.

I AM IN LOVE

"I am in love" is an expression shared by millions and maybe trillions every day on this earth. There is a sensation within the body that illuminates the heart, the mind, the body, and the soul. With its radiating power, someway, somehow it connects all the dots to the heart, mind, body, and soul. I am in love.

"I am in love" is a universal way of expressing how you feel about someone somewhere, and it is also a path to happiness. At least, in many ways, that is what we wish for and live for.

"I am in love with you, and you are in love with me" or "I love you" and "I love you too"—these are some of the most powerful words on this universe. Those words have been the catalyst to many long love affairs, marriages, creation of babies, and the bringing together of minds, hearts, souls, and spirits.

If it is true love, it becomes a part of your spirit. It can be so powerful that there is nothing on God's earth that can penetrate it.

"I am in love" can have such a soothing feeling within. "I am in love" will carry you up a hill, down a mountain, across the valley, and back again. The words "I love you"—when spoken softly, gently, with sincerity, with meaning, with excitement, and with the touch of your fingers—will make the spirit come alive not only for the moment, but also for a lifetime. "I am in love" and "I love you" are some of the most powerful words on this universe.

A GIFT FROM GOD

A gift from God can come from many sources, many vessels, and many avenues. It can bring love, happiness, quiet, and tranquility to the mind, body, heart, and soul.

A gift from God is like no other. It can come from nowhere. His vision you may not understand, but in time, God's vision shall be revealed. A gift from God is what we all live for.

A gift from God, accept it, cherish it, and be blessed from within your heart. He brings joy in the morning, afternoon, evening, all day, and all night long. Enjoy your gift.

BECAUSE OF YOU

Because of you, I do things that I have never experienced before. Because of you, my life is so beautiful and filled with a garden of red roses.

Because of you, I care so deeply, and my heart rejoices over and over for more of your love. Because of you, I realize life is more than just living. It's planning for every moment of the day with you.

Because of you, I dream of all the things I ever want to do and what I have thought I couldn't do. Because of you, my love grows and grows. And because of you, I see the rainbow surrounded by the warmth of the sunshine and the love from your heart. Because of you, you, and you.

GOD IS GOOD

God is good, no matter what your situation may be. Sometimes you laugh, you smile, and I joke; but other times, you cry, you hurt, and you wonder why. But God is good.

God is good because he has given me a gift—a gift that spans north, south, east, and west to show me things never seen or felt before and to understand life more and more. God is good.

In the midnight hour, when night has fallen and the mind is at rest, God is good because He is there with you regardless of your happiness, your pain, your joy, or your sadness; either way, God is good. I know my God, and I know He will not forsake you regardless. So I say to you, "God is good all the time."

SWEETHEART'S DAY

Sweetheart's Day for some folks is just another day with the same old routine, while Cupid strikes out and sets fire to the real lovers of the world.

Sweetheart's Day is for true lovers to smile, to cuddle, to express, to engage, to make hot, sexy love, and to enjoy each moment.

Sweetheart's Day is a day set aside to share all the great memories and send or receive candy and flowers. It's a day to say "I love you."

Sweetheart's Day is a true expression of real love without any doubt—love of today, love of tomorrow, and love of the flowers for each other. Just love, love, and love. Happy Sweetheart's Day to all the lovers in the world.

HAPPY SWEETHEART'S DAY

Love is in the air just about anywhere you look. Lovebirds are what they call them. I love you—these three powerful little words sometimes are more precious than gold, and other times, they can be dangerous and hurtful.

But on this day, love builds, love flows, love expands and repeats itself over and over. Happy Sweetheart's Day. Can it not be Sweetheart's Day every day?

LOVE—MY LIFE

You are my love and my life. One without the other, there is no love or life. I crave for you, your love, your smile, and your dreams, just to name a few, my darling.

I cannot conquer this world without you. So beautiful in your thoughts, so gentle in your touch, without you, I am nothing inside.

We have never realized how much real love means until we've met. Now I am yours, and you are mine, and together, the world belongs to us. Your love warms me inside and out. My love, my life belongs to you.

WHILE SITTING HERE

While sitting here, I am thinking of you and only you, the joy that you bring to my heart, mind, body, and soul. While sitting here, I am thinking of only you, the love that flows between two hearts, the expression that can only be expressed between us.

While sitting here, I am thinking of only you, the memories of you and only you. The memories of our love begin to flow north, south, east, and west. It reminds me of the Mississippi River.

While sitting here, I am thinking of you and only you. Just knowing how much you love me means so much, a love that cannot be duplicated. While sitting here, I am thinking of you and only you, the love of my life. Until next time. I love you.

It feels good to love you, to hold you, to touch you, to and say again, "I love you, baby." It feels good to love you because you care so deeply. You express your love so warmly. It feels good to love you knowing we have the greatest love God has ever given out.

It feels good to love you knowing my heart flutters for only you. It feels good to love you because of your warm smile, your sensitive touch, your beautiful deep eyes, and your forever expression of love. It feels good to love you every day of my life knowing my soul is at rest and my heart beats, and it beats for only you. It just feels good to love you and only you, my love.

I MISS YOU

I miss you in the morning, noon, and evening. I really miss you. I miss the sweetness of your voice, the gentleness of your touch, and the creativity of your mind. I miss you.

I miss you not because of anything extraspecial but because you are who you are. I miss that warm, radiant smile. I miss you like the sun in the sky, and the moon when it glows at night reminds me of you. I miss you.

I miss you because you are like a diamond that sparkles whether it's in the morning, at noon, or at night. I miss you.

I miss you because I can hear the softness in your voice repeatedly in my head saying, "I love you, and I miss you too." I miss you every day of my life, and knowing you are somewhere out there doing what needs to be done does not stop me from saying "I miss you."

I miss you, darling, because of all the things that you have done for me. I could make a list of the things that I have dreamed that you will do, and my list will be endless. I miss you.

You remind me of the ocean. If you could, imagine how big, wide, and deep the ocean is and I am in the middle thinking of nobody but you. I miss you now, and I always will miss you. I know I am surrounded by you every day of my life.

IF I NEVER LOVE AGAIN

If I never love again, I have loved you. If I never cry again, I have cried for you. If I never smile again, I have smiled for you. If I never touch again, I have touched you. If I never find peace, I have found it in you. If my world stopped still today, it would stop for you. If we could continue to love each other the way we do now, we will shatter the meaning of the word "love" into a thousand pieces.

If I could tell the world about my joy, my happiness, my strength, my love, my thoughts, my feelings, and my prayers, it would all be about you. We may be separated by a few miles, but our hearts are one. If we remain committed, the world belongs to *us*.

If I never feel this again, I have felt it all because of you. Written with much love, thought, and affection.

I TRIED TO CALL YOU UP

I tried to call you up on the phone, and all I got was "I am not accepting phone calls." You shattered my dreams, and you shattered my hopes. All I was trying to do was call you up.

I tried to call you up on the phone, and all I got was "I am not accepting phone calls." All I just wanted to tell you was that I was not being mean and just how sorry I was, but all I got when I tried to call you was "I am not accepting phone calls."

You shattered my dreams, and you shattered my hopes, but I would never give up, and I would keep trying for as long as I can because I wanted you to know that I tried to call you up.

I tried to call you up, but all I got was "I am not accepting phone calls." You shattered my dreams, and you shattered my hopes, but I would never ever give up.

I love you so much. I can't stop now, and I never will. I am going to keep trying because I know somewhere or somehow deep down within your heart that you know I love you and that I am truly sorry. I will send you a SOS of some kind to let you know it's time to accept my phone calls. Our love is deeper than not accepting my phone calls. I only want you to know I am not trying to be mean.

I love you with all my heart, and again, I am sorry. We have had a slight misunderstanding, and I am trying to clear up the confusion so that we can say to each other "I love you" and "I love you too." I have tried to call you up, and I am not giving up because within you is me, and within me is you.

IT'S TIME

It's time to say goodbye. Sometimes we have reasons to say goodbye, and other times, it is just the right thing to do. Saying goodbye does not mean that the person is gone forever. It means that there is another journey out there that they must complete.

It's okay to say goodbye when you stop by to chat because I already know you are just passing by.

Sometimes I can say goodbye with my heart, mind, body, and soul. There are other times when saying goodbye causes my mind, body, and soul to react like never before. If you have not been good to me and I have not been good to you, I am sure that I won't miss you.

So on this day, I want you to know it's okay to say goodbye because good love never ever dies. Once love becomes a part of the spirit, my presence and yours lives on and on.

JEALOUS

Jealousy can become very hurtful depending on the people involved. Because you want to be jealous without any basis, jealousy has no real place in the real world. However, it's a part of human life.

You are jealous because I am happy. You are jealous because I have more than you. You are jealous because I look better than you. You are jealous because of who I am and where I have come from or, better yet, where I am going.

Regardless of the situation, jealousy can be hurtful, and sometimes it's hard to understand why folks react, respond, or carry on like they do. Whatever you do in life, do not allow jealousy to consume your heart, mind, body, and soul. If you do, life will be a nightmare without any sunshine.

JUST ONE MORE THING

Life throws us a curve; sometimes we can straighten them out, and other times, we must deal with it. When we get up in the morning, we can't predict what might happen; but if it should go wrong, we say, "Just one more thing."

"Just one more thing" can be many, but for folks like me, it's just one more thing that God has given me to deal with. It's just one more thing.

Others, like me, must decide to stand tall, fold up, or run. I choose to stand tall. The old body is breaking down, but my spirit stands tall through it all. It's just one more thing. Just don't count me out. It's just one more thing that God has given me to deal with.

LOVE SHATTERS

Love shatters all plans, hopes, and dreams regardless of how much we desire otherwise. Our lives are built around love. Love to give, love to hope, love for the future, and love for humanity—it's just that universal word called "love."

Love can inspire new directions, new thoughts, new plans, and new deeper relationships. Love shatters.

Love can also destroy the core of who we are. It can shatter the best laid plans. It can divide a nation, cause conflicts, and destroy the best of relationships. Love shatters.

Love can heal the heart, mind, body, and soul. It can also heal things never thought of before. While love shatters, remember it can heal.

LOVE, RESPECT, HONESTY, AND HAPPINESS

Love, respect, honesty, trust, and happiness make a commitment between two people, and these are some of the most important ingredients in a relationship. We live for all these things to make the heart grow stronger, the mind clearer than water, the soul rest in peace, and the body rejoice as if it were Sunday in church.

We know when we have real love in our lives because we feel the feeling of two hearts as one. We know respect when it is obvious that we show each other that we care and love beyond reproach. Others on the outside can see without asking a question that respect is there.

We know honesty exists when there is no tension, no tears, and no crosswords and when you can feel within your gut that the truth is being spoken without any hidden stories. We are willing to share each other's whereabouts without hesitation, never giving the other person the impression through actions, eye contact, or sound of voice that the truth is not being told. Just sometimes all these things come into play in a relationship, most importantly not leaving one partner behind always or making things seem what they are not. Sharing, in this instance, always builds honesty that will live on when both partners are dead and gone. Finally, never be afraid to admit that you have made a mistake. God forgives, and so can you.

Happiness is a sure sign of contentment and pleasure. It has a way of displaying itself to the world in more ways than one. Happiness is like sunshine; you can't get enough. Happiness can make real lovers smile from coast to coast. Old eyes become new again. Happiness can make the heart beat faster than fast. Happiness, what a feeling! We live and die for the thought of real happiness, something no one can take from you.

Love, respect, honesty, and happiness combined into one can make life so much fun and enjoyable for eternity. Close your eyes and feel the feeling of love, respect, honesty, and happiness. These are just a few ingredients in a loving and caring relationship.

MIXED EMOTIONS

Mixed emotions can be both warm and loving or both infuriating and disappointing. Generally speaking, love is somewhere in the mix, and life experiences teach us that love can be good or not so good.

I love you without a doubt, but something is amiss, and I don't know why. You appear to be truthful, but something just doesn't feel right. Your body language is sending out mixed signals, your words are not as soft as they once have been, and that is causing me to have mixed emotions.

What am I to do when there are mixed emotions surrounding our relationship? Do I run, forget I am there, approach the situation head on, or just allow the situation to ride itself out. I am not sure. My love is there like always, but I can't take it anymore. Mixed emotions can destroy a relationship. If the emotions are clear, then the love gate can open, and my heart can love again, smile again, trust again, build again, romance again, and feel that I belong to you.

SOMETIMES WE SEE THE END

Sometimes we see the end of certain situations in life. It could be a job, school, relationships, or some other thing of importance in life.

Sometimes we see the end similar to "I see the writing on the wall." Life has a way of showing you what's about to happen or have taken place beforehand.

Sometimes we want to just say, "It's time to go. It's time to move on." Let's do something different, but it's time to go.

Sometimes folks feel the need to assist or push others to make a decision, so with that, we see the end. Sometimes when the end comes, some are sorry with regrets, and others rejoice in knowing the end is near.

Don't worry about me, for I am good. I have planned well, spent less money, and saved a lot, and now I am ready to move on to the next journey of life. Just sometimes we see the end of many things in life.

THINGS HAPPEN

For years, I have heard the expression "Things happen." I often wonder what that really means, but now I understand that things happen.

Life can be great—your smile, your thoughts, your intentions, and much more. All I can say is things happen.

Things happen sometimes without reasons; it can make the mind wander from left to right or up and down. Either way, things happen.

Things happen sometimes like a lightning rod, not sure where it might strike next. Things happen. For good or bad, things happen.

TIME AND LOVE HEAL EVERYTHING

"Love and time heal everything" is such a true statement. Without love, our lives will be nothing. Love and time heal everything when we feel our lives can't go on without love.

Sometimes love can shatter our hopes, our plans, and our dreams, but love and time heal everything. Love without time is like a dock without hands. Each has meaning in the world of love and time. Sometimes time and love feel like our enemy, but at the end of the day, love and time heal everything.

Thank you, love. Thank you, time. And together, love and time heal everything regardless of a person's situation.

WHAT IF I COULD LIVE THE REST OF MY LIFE WITH YOU?

What if I could live the rest of my life with you? I have dreamed living my life with you because of your sweet smile, your consideration, your concern, and all the things necessary that will make me want to live the rest of my life with you.

If I could live the rest of my life with you, would I want to? Yes, I would. You showed me love that I had never experienced before. You showed me how your touch meant so much. You showed me how your simple smile was an expression of you that lasted.

What if I could live the rest of my life with you? I will feel like I am in heaven too. Your gentleness is an aspiration for the mind, and your calmness soothes my heart, body, mind, and soul.

What if I could live the rest of my life with you? Will I? Yes, I will because you have given me new ways at looking at life, new ways of thinking about the past, the present, and the future. You have brought me to a place where I know I am secure—secure in your smile, in your thoughts, in your eyes, in your heart, and in your soul.

What if I could live the rest of my life with you? Will I? Yes, I will. To be so certain and confident about you is a revelation of sort because it translates the mind, the body, the soul, the spirit to a place where they have never been before.

Sometimes we fail to stop and think about what we have and what we could do to enhance the quality of our relationship and our lives. The question remains, what if I could live the rest of my life with you? Will I? Yes, I will to the very end.

You are my love, my heart, my inspiration, and you are the person of my dreams.

WHAT IF I DIDN'T HAVE YOU IN MY LIFE?

What if I didn't have you in my life? Where would I be? And on this day, I have no clue where I would be. What if I was floating in the ocean on a raft, just wondering if I could or would make it?

What if you were not in my life? I have wondered that a million times, and I still don't know where I would be. What if you were not in my life?

What if you were not in my life? Would I be able to smile, laugh, cry, plan for tomorrow, and look forward to another day? I just don't know where I would be.

What if I didn't have you in my life? All I can say to the world today is that if you were not in my life, I would be like the person in the raft in the ocean just floating, hoping really that I would be rescued by someone as sweet, loving, and caring as you.

What if I didn't have you in my life? I would hope that I would never ever have to answer that question.

WHAT'S NEXT?

What's next in the life of the human race when love has a lot to be desired?

One day things are so wonderful, and then the next day, something new emerges, and we have to ask, what's next?

"Life" and "love" is an amazing combination of words; mixed together, they can be exciting, and then it can be a nightmare, not sure how this is going to roll out. We hope for the best, and then the worst happens.

It's almost like a pan of boiling water. Sometimes you have to allow it to cool down before you make your next decision or move. You never know what's next.

Life is so interesting that we will wonder about what's next in the life of the human race when love has so much to be desired. What's next?

WHY HAS IT COME TO THIS?

Why has it come to this? I don't know. Voices are raised, eyebrows are raised, blood is flowing, and the thoughts of everything go every which way.

Why has it come to this? There has been so much love between us, back and forth, back and forth, and now the smiles are gone, the laughter is gone, and all that's left is tension. So again, why has it come to this?

I am told no matter the situation, I am the problem, or it is my fault? Could it not be our fault? After years of loving each other, now my appearance all of a sudden is causing an issue. I don't understand. Why has it come to this?

Our future is on the line. I am tired of all the stress and the blame toward me instead of sharing the love, the pain, the ups and downs.

My heart, mind, body, and soul just can't take it anymore. Where have we gone wrong? Is it over? Where are we headed next, and again, why has it come to this? I am numb.

A HOLE IN MY SOUL

Every man and woman at some time and place has had a hole in their soul. A hole in my soul can be very deep. A hole to hold on to or a hole to fall into—either way, I have a hole in my soul.

Could it be from life experiences like living and loving? I just don't know. But what I do know is that there is a hole in my soul.

I search every day and in every way that I know how to close that hole that's in my soul. Could it be that I am not sure exactly what I am feeling? Or could it be from lack of love, happiness, inspiration, trust, faith, family, and friends or just a feeling that there is a hole in my soul? In some place somewhere, that hole that's in my soul will be filled with so much joy that my mind, heart, and soul will forget that I have ever had a hole in my soul..

Live life to the best of your ability and share love daily, and I can assure you that you will never ever have another hole in your soul. With love.

YOUR UNDERSTANDING OF ME IS FADING

You have brought me out of the darkness into the light, and now your understanding of me is fading, and I don't understand why.

Years, it seems, have passed me by with such understanding of love, happiness, trust, companionship, and much more, yet my mind feels I am being left behind when the road leads north. It appears and feels like a blast from the past, and that is never good in the mind of someone recovering from use and abuse. Maybe it's all in the mind.

The words "I am sorry" seems to have less meaning as the road leads north and south. What is it going to take to stop this fading of your understanding of me? From the darkness of life to the joy of the heart, mind, body, and soul, wanting to never let go of love and happiness.

Your understanding of me is fading, and I don't understand why. Don't lose the best thing God has given us, for we may never see it again.

I can only travel this road once, and that once is now. The mind is tired, and the soul is not far behind. Joy has been the greatest inspiration of today, tomorrow, and the future, so has the light. Let's leave the world shining upon love, life, happiness, joy, and inspiration and not this—your understanding of me is fading, and I don't understand why.

IS THERE PEACE?

Love and lies do not mix regardless of how small or big the lie is. Days of fighting become weeks, and true love comes into question. It's like quicksand; slowly, things begin to sink, but just how far is determined by if someone gives you a lifeline.

Fighting destroys the fiber of any foundation, regardless of how strong or weak it may be. We dream of that true love that carries us to a heavenlike state or one that protects us from all evil. Love is what sustains us in time of happiness, in time of despair, and in time when there is no time.

Peace and trust becomes the cornerstone of rebuilding what has been shattered. Peace will ease the heart, mind, body, and soul. Trust will show you that I have made a mistake, but I can show you that I have learned from it. Trust can rebuild love, faith, and understanding and can give a relationship a new beginning.

TRUST

"Trust" is a powerful word in our universe that means so much to our everyday living. Trust is giving your word of honesty. Without trust, our lives are really shattered. We trust those whom we love and expect trust in return.

Trust between people is the secret and is reassuring to the heart, body, mind, and soul. When trust is broken between two people, regardless of their relationship, it can be devastating to those involved and to the relationship. Broken trust can be shocking to the mind, heart, and emotions.

Broken trust is not the end of the world, especially if you really love someone. The person responsible must be willing to accept responsibility for their actions, express true remorse, and begin to show to the other person that they can be trusted again.

Broken trust is like a person's broken word. Your word is your bond, and if you break your bond, your word is worthless. So if you find yourself in a situation where trust is broken and you love that person, do whatever it takes to make it right.

Trust can be rebuilt, but you must work on it. Again, it is not the end of the world, but don't make that mistake ever again. True love is always worth fighting for. Be blessed for what you have and not what you think is around the corner.

Trust is for a lifetime. Honor your word. Love and enjoy life. God will have wanted it that way.

I AM NOTHING WITHOUT YOU

I am nothing without you. My life begins and will end with you; that's what real love is all about. I am nothing without you because so much of my happiness comes from you, and with God in our lives, we can't go wrong.

I am nothing without you. You inspire me in so many ways that my heart rejoices from your mere presence in my life. I am nothing without you. I pray every day that our love continues to grow for each other.

I am nothing without you. You give me strength when I am weak. You give me the lift when I need uplifting. You give me so much love, respect, and honor, and belief in you gives me the strength to believe in myself. I am nothing without you.

CONFUSION

I think I know what I want, and there is confusion. I think it's right, and I discover it's wrong, but there's confusion. I see things, and I need and purchase things I want, but there's confusion.

I dream of the make-believe and see the impossible, but there is confusion. I read and think that I know what it means, but there is confusion. I reach out my hand to help, but there is confusion. I give my heart totally, but there is confusion. I attempt to love, and there is confusion.

I ask simple questions, but there is confusion. No matter what life has to offer, there is confusion. So in the end, disregard confusion because it is confused with confusion, thus making everything confused. Be happy, be loved, be cared for, be respected, and never be confused.

I'M SORRY

I have written a poem titled "I Am Sorry." My thoughts still hold true. I am sorry for what I have done to you. I have given you the best years of my life, and the love has just faded away.

I am sorry for no longer being in love with you, but I will always love you for the wonderful years we have shared. You may never forgive me, but I am sorry.

Life must go on despite what has happened. We believe in God, and He will forgive us for our sins. He will heal our broken hearts and mend our rattled souls. I am sorry our love has faded away.

Thank you for all the years that we have been together. I am sorry for what I could not fix. It is not your fault, and it is not mine either. You know it was over long ago. It is time to let go. May you find it in your heart to forgive me.

LOVE AND LIES DO NOT MIX

Love and lies do not mix. Sometimes and for some unknown reasons, people have a true tendency to lie. They lie because it is fun, lie because they do not know how to tell you, or just because it is their nature.

Either way, when a person is in love with another person for whatever reason and they put their hearts into making sure the other knows they are loved and they believe the other person to know no end, then a lie pops up from nowhere, and it is a confirmed lie, and then the fireworks begin to pop, pop, and pop. Love and lies do not mix.

Love itself can be a powerful solution to many things in a human being's life. I have seen it cure the incurable, I have seen it make a person smile who has not smiled in years, I have seen love make a person want to live again and enjoy it. However, love and lie do not mix.

Sad to say, love and lies have caused many people to die early or become injured severely and even spend the rest of their life behind bars. The mind is a terrible thing to waste no matter what the situation may be. But when a person's emotions are involved, sometimes they fail to understand reason. Love and lies do not mix.

Love is when touching someone makes your heart go wild and gives you that sense of security that you are somebody and that you belong to someone very special. Love is really a wonderful thing when it is applied in the right purpose.

Lies can be so destructive that it can tear down a wall that has stood for years, destroy a relationship that has been built on honesty, and shatter the best of the best, the strongest of the strongest between men and women. Lie, what a destructive thing.

Love and lies do not mix. The mind sometimes can snap if a person is not careful and has no one to vent to, building up inside like a volcanic eruption that will not end its lava flow, just building and building.

While the human mind can bear a lot of bad things, the mind and the heart can recover and become even stronger but only when love is restored to a stronger level than before the cracks begin to show.

Love is more powerful than anything in this world because God is love. So you have to learn to love and appreciate it to its finest hour. Enjoy each minute, each hour, each day, each week, or each year as if it would be your last day on the earth. True love never dies. A new love with a new experience can make life feel like a newborn baby, a love that you can feel even when you are not near that person.

Never allow a second go by without saying to yourself, "I love that person more than life itself." The feeling of being close to someone, the feeling of knowing you are the only one that they love and need and no one else can penetrate that barrier of love that surrounds you.

Each day when you think of that person, a smile of happiness appears on your face, never a wrinkle, just a smile of love and happiness. Love and lies do not mix. It's like dynamite; something is going to explode, and that is not what love is supposed to be about.

Love and lies do not mix, and it can shatter lives that otherwise won't be shattered. Love and lies can affect more than the folks involved, especially if a tragedy takes place. Be honest and be true, and you will always prevail in real love.

Love and lies do not mix, but when it comes together, you think in these terms: You are in love with that person who makes you happier than you have ever been in your life. You look forward to the day that you are surrounded with love twenty-four hours a day, seven days a week for the rest of your life. That's an indication that your heart, mind, body, and soul belong to that person. Love and lies do not mix. Enjoy life; it's the only one you will ever have.

Cedar Point
303 Yards →

GOD FORGIVES

The Almighty God forgives us for our sins. He knows and understands our hearts. God knows our moves, intentions, and thoughts. God forgives.

We sometimes get caught up into something that can create so much pain and confusion that we can't find a way out. Pray to God, and He will guide you through the hills and valleys. God forgives.

Sometimes God places people in our lives for a reason, and in time, His reason is unveiled. Trust in the Lord knowing He forgives.

You must believe Jesus is the Son and confess your sins; try to live by His Word. We are all His children through the good times and the bad times. God forgives.

WHO AM I TO JUDGE?

Who am I to judge if one is right or wrong? So often we are so quick to inflict a judgment before we even know what is right or wrong and before we know the entire story. So who am I to judge?

Who am I to judge whether it be about life, love, family, friends, and many other situations? That is the question. We often judge without even knowing the facts. So who am I to judge?

Who am I to judge your choices in life? It is not for me to judge. So often we are on the outside looking in, trying to put two and two together and always coming up short, but we are so quick to inflict judgment. So I ask, who am I to judge?

Who am I to judge about anything in life but myself? If we can learn not to judge others, then the world will be a much better place. We are so often asked for an opinion. An opinion often leads to premature judgments, and when we find ourselves judging others about the same thing that we have done in life, we somehow forget that we have done some of the same things or even worse. So I ask, who am I to judge?

To judge is not for me. We all know someday we are all going to transcend from this life to the next life, our judgment will come before the Lord. Yet we are judged so harshly sometimes by others who don't even know the story. They don't even know the punch line. They don't even know the characters in the scene. They know nothing except a tongue that wags and wags.

I say to those out there, before you choose to judge, look at yourself in the mirror; and if you can say that you are perfect, then maybe, just maybe, you have the right to judge. However, it is my belief that neither you nor I have the right to judge. So who am I to judge?

CPSIA information can be obtained
at www.ICGtesting.com
Printed in the USA
BVHW021031260219
541199BV00026B/1192/P